Copyright for Photographers
Christa Laser
Copyright © 2013 Christa Laser. All rights reserved.
CreateSpace Edition.
Published in the United States.

Disclaimer: The materials available in this book are for informational purposes only and not for the purpose of providing legal advice. You should contact your attorney to obtain advice with respect to any particular issue or problem. Because law varies by jurisdiction, is subject to interpretation, and changes over time, the information contained herein may not be accurate in your situation. Use of this book does not create an attorney-client relationship. The opinions expressed herein are the opinions of Christa Laser alone and do not reflect the opinions of Kirkland & Ellis LLP. Where external materials are cited, linked, or quoted, such a citation is not an endorsement and those materials reflect the opinions of the content's author alone and might not reflect the opinion of Christa Laser or Kirkland & Ellis LLP. No copyright is claimed in official U.S. government works, such as copyright laws quoted herein.

CONTENTS

Introduction 1

U.S. Copyright Basics 2

    What is a copyright? 2

    Who owns a copyright? 2

    When does a copyright exist? 4

    What is the effect of registration? 4

    What is the effect of a copyright notice? 8

    Chapter recap 10

Photographs of Landscapes, Still Life, and Nature 12

Photographs of Statues and Third Party Works 14

Photographs of People 17

    Basics of Rights of Publicity 17

    Basics of Rights of Privacy 19

    Basics of False Light 21

    What is a release? 22

Licensing Basics 24

    What is a license? If I license a photograph, do I still own it? 24

    What is a Creative Commons License and how does it work? 25

Fair Use 27

Remedies in the United States 30

    Cease and Desist 30

    DMCA Notice 32

Photography Abroad 34

Conclusion 35

References 36

    Copyright laws 36

    Other helpful websites 51

About the Author 52

INTRODUCTION

Photographers are not only artists. They live in a web of laws that define the scope of their rights and their business. Those who understand the laws applicable to them can develop and monetize their art with less risk. But photographers who do not have a basic understanding of the law can become victims of it.

This short book is designed to give photographers some of the initial background information that they need to better understand the laws applicable to them. This book focuses on U.S. copyright, rights of privacy, rights of publicity, and contract law, so photographers from other countries should be careful to contact their attorney to help understand whether similar rules are applicable where they live. The information in this book cannot substitute for the advice of your attorney, but hopefully it provides helpful insight.

U.S. COPYRIGHT BASICS

WHAT IS A COPYRIGHT?

Let's begin by defining a copyright. A copyright is a right that allows the copyright holder to stop other people from copying, selling, displaying, or creating derivations of a work without permission. In other words, it is a right to exclude.

Contrary to popular belief, a copyright is not a right for the copyright holder to use the work. In fact, as will be explored in later chapters, other people can have conflicting rights in a work that prevent the copyright holder from using the work (such as a model's right to control the use of her image or an artist's copyright in art appearing in the work).

WHO OWNS A COPYRIGHT?

Most of the time, the person who creates the work is the one who owns the copyright. Therefore, a photographer who takes an image will usually be the copyright holder of that image. If more than one person participates creatively in a single work, the default rule is that all the contributors to the work share the copyright as co-authors and have equal rights to the profits generated from the work.

One common exception to the rule of the creator as the copyright holder is a "work made for hire." A work can be made for hire either if it is prepared by an employee as part of his or her employment or, in the case of certain limited categories of work like a contribution to a collective artistic project, if the parties agree in writing that the work will be considered a work made for hire. If a work is made for hire, the employer, not the artist, will own the copyright as soon as it is created.

Additionally, if you are working as an independent contractor on a project where the work for hire doctrine does not apply, your contractor agreement might still include a clause where you agree to "assign" or "transfer" your copyrights. What this typically means is that you are agreeing that even though you own the copyright to begin with, you give over ownership of that copyright upon its creation. In the short term, this kind of agreement has a similar effect to a work for hire situation, because in both cases you will no longer be the copyright holder of your work and will not be entitled to enforce your copyright. The primary difference, however, is that the creator of a work has the right to cancel an "assignment" or "transfer" of a copyright, typically after 35 years, whereas a work for hire belongs to an employer for the entire copyright term.

WHEN DOES A COPYRIGHT EXIST?

Any original artistic work, like a photograph, is protectable under copyright law as soon as it is fixed in a tangible medium of expression. This means any form from which the work can be seen, copied, or communicated. In the case of a photograph, a copyright is formed as soon as the image is captured.

WHAT IS THE EFFECT OF REGISTRATION?

While a copyright exists as soon as the work is fixed, there are certain benefits that are only available to those who register their copyright. Most importantly, if you register your copyright prior to the start of the infringement of the work or within three months of publication, you will be entitled to seek statutory damages and attorney's fees.

Statutory damages are damages that are defined by the Copyright Act as an optional alternative to collecting for the actual harm you suffered and the profits earned by the infringer (called "actual damages"). Statutory damages typically range between $750 and $30,000, but they can be increased to up to $150,000 in the case of willful infringement (for example, when the infringer knows that they are violating your copyright) or decreased to no less than $200 in the case innocent infringement (if the infringer was not aware and had no reason to believe that the use infringed a copyright). You as the copyright holder, presuming you registered in time to be entitled to statutory damages, have the right to decide whether you want to seek actual or statutory damages. Many copyright holders prefer statutory damages because, unlike with actual damages, the copyright holder does not need to offer evidence of actual monetary harm or actual profits earned by the infringer in order to collect a damage award. On the other hand, there could be a situation in which the infringer earned far more than $150,000 off of your work, in which case you might decide, in consultation with your attorney, to seek actual damages instead.

 Copyright registration is also critical in other ways. Before you can file a lawsuit for infringement of a copyright, you have to register the copyright. Registration also serves as evidence in court of important things like ownership of the copyright and the identity of the creator of the work and carries heavy weight when it is filed within five years of publication. Attorneys typically urge all photographers to register their work in a timely fashion, either prior to publication or within three months of publication.

 A single registration can include multiple photos. Unpublished photos, regardless of when they were created, can be registered together if the same photographer took all the photos and all the photos have the same copyright holder. If you register a work when it is unpublished, you do not need to re-register it once it is published. Published photos can be registered in a single group application if all the photos were published in the same calendar year, if the same photographer took all the photos, and if all the photos have the same copyright holder. Online copyright registration (for a group of unpublished photos at http://www.copyright.gov/eco/) costs $35, while paper filing (for a group of published photos on form http://www.copyright.gov/forms/formgr_pph_con.pdf) cost $65 at the time this was written (though be aware that the Copyright Office has noted that it might raise rates sometime in 2014). The Copyright Office website provides instructions along with each application to guide you through the process, or you can call the Copyright Office at 1-877-476-0778.

WHAT IS THE EFFECT OF A COPYRIGHT NOTICE?

A copyright notice—that mark appearing on a work that specifies the copyright status, the year of publication, and the author, e.g., © 2013 Christa Laser—is no longer required by U.S. law. Nonetheless, there are some legal benefits of continuing to use a copyright notice.

First, when an infringer of a copyrighted work does not know that the work is protected and has no reason to believe that the use infringes a copyright, the damages that infringer must pay might be lowered. This is called "innocent infringement." While innocent infringement is difficult to show, and while there are other ways for photographers to tell potential infringers that the work is protected, federal law states that innocent infringement does not apply if works have a copyright notice. In other words, using a copyright notice will ensure that the copyright holder's damages are not reduced due to innocent infringement.

Second, it can be a violation of the Digital Millennium Copyright Act ("DMCA") to intentionally remove copyright information, knowing that doing so will enable or conceal infringement. This law extends not just to copyright notices themselves, but includes other identifying information conveyed along with the work such as the title of the work, the name of the photographer, contact information for the photographer, terms of use or symbols identifying those terms (e.g., Creative Commons licensing marks), or other information. Damages typically range from $2,500 to $25,000 per violation. Therefore, another benefit of using a copyright notice (or, in this case, other identifying information) in connection with your work is to potentially entitle you to damages under the DMCA for intentional removal of copyright information.

Use of a copyright notice is a personal decision. Those who do not want to place a copyright notice on their work, but who are concerned about innocent infringement, might wish to use other methods to identify themselves to as many people as possible, such as by providing their name and terms of use in text appearing below their images. Keep in mind, however, that such information might not be as effective as a copyright notice appearing on the work.

CHAPTER RECAP

These are some of the key lessons you should take away from this chapter:

- A copyright is a right to exclude.
- The creator of the photo is generally the copyright holder. This can change if the photo is a "work for hire" or if you sign an agreement "assigning" or "transferring" your copyright.
- A copyright in a photo exists as soon as the image is captured.
- Copyright registration can provide access to statutory damages, is a prerequisite to a lawsuit, and can serve as evidence in a lawsuit.

- A copyright notice is not required, but can help you fight against claims of innocent infringement and can entitle you to damages under the DMCA if anyone intentionally removes your notice in an attempt to infringe your work.

PHOTOGRAPHS OF LANDSCAPES, STILL LIFE, AND NATURE

Landscapes, still life, and nature are the lowest risk—legally, at least—of all the types of photography. Unlike photographs of artwork or people, you are unlikely to face legal claims from third parties when you try to publish your work. Rather, the most common concern that landscape, still life, and nature photographers face is whether they are allowed to go onto certain property to take photographs and what sorts of items they are allowed to bring when they do so.

Under trespass laws, a private property owner may restrict you from entering onto his or her property to take photographs. Even public spaces, like state or national parks, may restrict certain types of photography (such as commercial photography) or use of certain equipment (such as a tripod) without a permit. There are, however, certain First Amendment protections of your right to photograph in highly public spaces like public sidewalks or to photograph newsworthy events like fires or other disasters from public spaces.

PHOTOGRAPHS OF STATUES AND THIRD PARTY WORKS

Like photographs, other works of art such as statues are frequently protected by a copyright. Furthermore, a person might infringe a copyright in other's artwork not only by making an exact copy of the work, but also by reproducing images of the work in the form of a photograph. In other words, when you publish a photograph of someone else's work, you risk being held liable for infringement of that person's copyright.

For example, the copyright holders of statues frequently assert their rights against people who publish photographs of their work—a fact that might surprise you. This can be true even for statues that are located in public spaces. Many statues located in public spaces have been claimed to be protected by copyright, including the Korean War Memorial in Washington, D.C., where a lawsuit was filed for copyright infringement over photographs of the Memorial appearing on U.S. Postage Stamps, and the Wall Street Bull, where a lawsuit was filed for copyright infringement over photographs of the Bull appearing on the cover of a book. Some copyrights in statues have been formally dedicated to public domain, meaning that copyright law no longer applies to restrict the use of images of those statues. Some other statues have expired copyrights because the work was created many years ago. It can be difficult to determine on your own when a statue is protected by copyright, so because copyrights are granted automatically upon creation and can last for many years, it is usually best to assume that a statue is protected by copyright, even if it is located in a public space, and to not publish photographs of the statue without first getting the permission of the copyright holder.

Street art is also often copyright-protected. As with statues, publishing a photograph of street art can violate copyright law. A copyright to a work can exist even if a work is not signed by the artist and, as noted in the discussion about statues, even if it is publicly displayed. Therefore, you should always get permission from the street artist before publishing photographs of their work. Inability to locate the creator of the street art does not excuse you from liability for copyright infringement under current law (though Congress is considering possible "orphan works legislation" that could limit copyright liability where the artist cannot be located and certain other requirements are satisfied, *if* the legislation is ultimately passed into law).

For both statues and street art, as well as other artists' works that might appear in photos, photographers sometimes believe that their use of the work was a "fair use." However, as discussed in the section below on fair use, there are many factors that a court will consider in deciding whether a use is a fair use. Frequently, photographers who take photos of another artist's work are held liable for copyright infringement.

PHOTOGRAPHS OF PEOPLE

Individuals who appear in your photos have rights to their image, name, and privacy that can interfere with your ability to capture, publish, and sell your photos. The laws applicable to photographs of people are often state laws that can vary from region to region, so you should always ask your attorney for advice if you are trying to use someone's image without their permission. The sections below merely provide an introduction to some of the laws that might arise.

BASICS OF RIGHTS OF PUBLICITY

The right of publicity is the right of each person to control the commercial use of their likeness (meaning their image) and their name. The right of publicity is a state law cause of action. Therefore, the scope of the right will differ from state to state. In most cases, courts will apply the law of the state where the subject of the photograph lives. For example, if you take photographs of a model who lives in New York, New York law might apply to determine the scope of the right of publicity.

New York is a common place for model and street photography and has a relatively strong right of publicity law. In New York, the state law proscribes that no one can use another person's name or likeness "for advertising or for purposes of trade" without the person's consent. While photographers are often aware that this law can apply to magazines and billboards used to advertise products, they often are not aware that the law occasionally has been read to extend to displays and sales of the photograph itself. For example, a federal appellate court applying New York law previously held that a detachable poster depicting wrestlers that was included inside a magazine violated the wrestlers' right of publicity.

There are exceptions to New York's right of publicity law, though. In one case, a New York court held that a street photographer could use stylized photos of people taken in a public place in a book and exhibits, all without the consent of the subjects of those photographs, because the photos were artistic expressions protected by freedom of speech. Additionally, use of someone's image for the purpose of reporting a "newsworthy" event is also frequently exempt from this law; some celebrity street photographers argue that the "newsworthiness" exception applies to celebrity photos published in gossip magazines, as the public has a demand for news about celebrities' activities.

Many other states also restrict the right to use someone's name or image without consent. The scope of the right, however, and the way that courts have interpreted what exceptions apply, varies depending on what state's law is applicable.

BASICS OF RIGHTS OF PRIVACY

One rule that can prevent a photographer from capturing a photo of a person is the right to privacy, and specifically the right to be free from intrusion into private spaces. There are many environments in which people might have a reasonable expectation that they will not be photographed, such as when they are in dressing rooms, when they are entering their ATM pin code, or when they are in their bedroom. Photographers who take photographs of people in these situations might be held liable for invasion of those people's privacy. Note, simply because a bedroom or bathroom window is visible from a public place like a sidewalk does not mean that the photographer has a right to take photographs.

Another privacy right is the right to be free from public disclosure of private facts. In many states, a publisher is liable for disclosure of private facts where the disclosure would be highly offensive to a reasonable person and where the public has no legitimate interest in the information. For example, some people might argue that photographs of a person suffering from a medical condition in private or nude photographs taken in private that are then published to a wider audience could be considered a violation of the right to be free from public disclosure of private facts. When you take photographs, you should be mindful of other people's privacy.

BASICS OF FALSE LIGHT

In some states, people appearing in photographs may sue if the photograph depicts them in a "false light." Although, like other state law causes of action, the rule differs from state to state, many states that permit this cause of action require the person appearing in the photo to show: (1) the photograph depicts the person in a false light, such as in a way that suggests something untrue about the person; (2) the false light in which the person was placed would be highly offensive to a reasonable person, meaning it would be reasonable for an ordinary person to be very upset about being depicted in that way; and (3) the person who published the photograph must have known the depiction was not accurate or acted with reckless disregard of the truth.

Lawsuits for false light are increasingly common, perhaps because of increased use of stock photography and licensed photos instead of dedicated photo shoots for each advertisement. There has been a recent wave of lawsuits, for example, after an HIV-support advertisement used models' images purchased from a stock photography website in a way that falsely suggested that the models have HIV. There are many less egregious cases where the law against false light could also be applied. Therefore, it is best to publish photos that accurately portray the models in your photo.

WHAT IS A RELEASE?

A "release" is an agreement that photographers may obtain from a model or other person appearing in a photograph that releases the photographer from potential liability for use of the person's image or name in connection with the photograph. Releases can be written in a way that prevents models or other people in the photograph from succeeding in lawsuits claiming a violation of their rights to their image. Sample model releases are available online or through organizations such as the American Society of Media Photographers (http://asmp.org/tutorials/adults-model-release.html), though you should always consult with your attorney to make sure that the release is adequate for you.

LICENSING BASICS

WHAT IS A LICENSE? IF I LICENSE A PHOTOGRAPH, DO I STILL OWN IT?

There is an important distinction between a license and a transfer. When you give someone a license, you are giving them permission to use your work, but a license does not transfer ownership of the copyright in the work. A license can be either "exclusive" or "non-exclusive." A non-exclusive license gives the other person the right to use your work, but does not give the other person the right to stop you from using your work or authorizing others to use it. An exclusive license gives the other person the sole right to use your work, meaning that you cannot continue to use your work and you cannot authorize others to do so, even though you still own the copyright.

A transfer of copyright means that you no longer own the copyright to your work and all of your rights to exclude or to license will pass to the person who purchased the copyright. Note that there are provisions built into the Copyright Act to protect artists from unintentionally transferring their copyright. For example, contracts transferring copyrights must be signed and in writing. Additionally, the Copyright Act contains provisions allowing artists to cancel transfers and licenses after 35 years by following certain steps.

WHAT IS A CREATIVE COMMONS LICENSE AND HOW DOES IT WORK?

A Creative Commons license is a tool that enables you to tell the public that you are granting them a non-exclusive license to your work. You might choose to use a Creative Commons license, for example, if you want your fans to be able to copy your work and share it with their friends under terms that you choose. Many popular photographers use Creative Commons licenses to increase distribution of their work. There are many types of Creative Commons licenses to choose from if you are interested in providing the public with access to your work (available here: http://creativecommons.org/licenses/). A popular license is the Attribution Non-Commercial license, which allows members of the public to use your work non-commercially as long as they give you credit every time they use it. In deciding whether to use a Creative Commons license, you should keep in mind that granting a Creative Commons license can interfere with your ability to grant exclusive licenses to others in the future and can decrease the value of your copyright in the event your want to sell your copyright at a later time. Nonetheless, such licenses can be a creative tool to gain wider audiences for your work.

FAIR USE

While a copyright generally gives the copyright holder a right to exclude others from using a work, there are some limits on that right, including the defense of "fair use." Sometimes, another person's use of your photograph might be fair use, entitling that person to use your photograph without your permission. Other times, you might be trying to use a third party's work, such as if you use a portion of another artist's work in your own, and will be trying to claim that your use is fair use.

The purpose of fair use is to make sure that copyright law is not used as a means to restrict speech, including criticism, comment, news reporting, or education. Considerations in a fair use analysis include such factors as whether the use transforms the original in a way that gives it a different meaning, whether the use is for non-profit educational purposes, whether only an insignificant portion of the work is being used for a short period of time, and whether the use of the work will impact the market for or value of the copyrighted work.

Some photographers incorrectly believe that fair use gives them the right to publish photographs of statues or street art without the permission of the artist. In most cases, merely publishing a photograph of another person's work does not "transform" the work and is not a fair use unless there are other factors at play. A federal court has held, for example, that a photograph of the Korean War Memorial statues used on postage stamps violated the sculptor's copyright and was not a transformative fair use, even though the photograph incorporated additional creative elements like dramatic angles and a surrealistic tone.[1]

A few photographers also incorrectly believe that if they are not selling or making money from a particular photograph, then they are making a fair use of third party works that may appear in the photo, like statues

---

[1] *Gaylord v. United States*, 595 F.3d 1364 (Fed. Cir. 2010).

and art. However, offering a photo to the public for free can negatively impact the market for a work appearing in the photo, such as by decreasing the price people are willing to pay to view the work. Non-commercial use is only one of many factors in the fair use analysis, so photographers should be cautious about using third party works without permission even if they will not make money from the photo.

Deciding whether use of a work is a fair use is a complicated, fact-intensive process. Law on fair use can differ depending on the court deciding the issue and the unique facts of the situation. Therefore, like with other copyright issues, photographers should be cautious about trying to analyze fair use without the assistance of an attorney.

REMEDIES IN THE UNITED STATES

While photographers are frequently aware of the option to bring a lawsuit to remedy a violation of their copyright, some are not aware of other options for resolving the dispute, including sending a letter asking infringers to cease and desist their activities or issuing a DMCA takedown notice in the case of online infringement.

CEASE AND DESIST

A "cease and desist" letter is a letter telling an infringer that you believe they are infringing your copyright and asking the infringer to stop their activities. A cease and desist letter can be a useful tool to engage in conversation or negotiation with someone who has used your photograph without permission. In many cases, the parties can amicably settle copyright infringement claims through this kind of communication without resorting to a lawsuit.

However, a cease and desist letter carries risks and should only be written in consultation with an attorney. One of the biggest risks is the potential for an unwanted lawsuit; the United States has a law called the Declaratory Judgment Act that frequently permits a person who receives your cease and desist letter to file a lawsuit to get guidance about whether there was in fact a violation of your copyright. The primary factor influencing whether infringers can bring a declaratory judgment lawsuit is whether your letter, in light of the circumstances of infringement, gives them a real and reasonable fear that you might sue them. Because the person who files the lawsuit gets to choose the court where the lawsuit will be heard and because the interpretation of laws can differ in each region, a declaratory judgment lawsuit often throws a significant monkey wrench into your legal strategy. In sum, it is important for you to work closely with an attorney to evaluate the risks of a potential lawsuit and whether there is a way, in your situation, to structure your negotiations with a potential infringer so as to limit your risk of such a lawsuit.

DMCA NOTICE

The Digital Millennium Copyright Act ("DMCA") includes a provision that encourages internet service providers to remove information that they have been notified infringes a copyright. As a result of this provision, copyright holders can often obtain removal of infringing content from the web without filing a lawsuit and without even registering the copyright. The notice that the copyright holder provides to the internet service provider is called a "DMCA takedown notice." The DMCA specifies that the notice must include your name, contact information, a physical or electronic signature, an identification of the copyrighted work that was infringed, an identification of the material that is infringing, a statement that you have a good faith belief that use of the material in the manner complained of violates your copyright, and a statement that the information in your notification is accurate and "under penalty of perjury" that you are the holder (or authorized to act on behalf of the holder) of the copyright that is allegedly infringed. It is recommended that you contact your attorney for advice about whether the use infringes or is fair use before you file a notice.

Most content-hosting websites have an option or link near the content to report copyright infringement or support pages on copyright infringement that tell you where to submit your notice. In the case of independent websites that post infringing content, you can look up the name and contact information of the domain host online.[2]

---

[2] Starting sometime in 2014, the non-profit organization ICANN should have a search service available at http://whois.icann.org/. In the meantime, other websites also provide "Whois" searches. For additional information about how to find an internet service provider using a "Whois" search, visit the following web post on the subject: http://www.naturescapes.net/articles/business/using-the-dmca-takedown-notice-to-battle-copyright-infringement/.

PHOTOGRAPHY ABROAD

International treaties have attempted to harmonize many aspects of copyright law around the world, meaning that copyright laws can be similar in several respects in many developed countries and a copyright formed in one country is often enforceable in another. However, despite these treaties, not all aspects of copyright law are the same. For example, some countries provide additional "moral rights" to artists, and some do not have the same rules as the United States regarding when certain remedies are available for copyright infringement. Additionally, some rights of third parties, in particular the right of privacy, are largely not subject to these international treaties. Accordingly, they often vary dramatically from country to country. Non-U.S. photographers who are reading this book and photographers publishing works in a foreign country are advised to contact a local attorney to learn more about the applicable laws.

CONCLUSION

Are you beginning to understand some parts of the laws that make up the web you walk as a photographer? Hopefully, this book provided you with an introduction that will help you make the most of your art and avoid some common risks.

Remember, because laws are applied differently depending on your situation, you should always contact an attorney with your legal concerns. For those who cannot afford an attorney, there are local legal aid programs dedicated to providing artists with access to legal services, such as New York's Volunteer Lawyers for the Arts, D.C.'s Washington Area Lawyers for the Arts, and Chicago's Lawyers for the Creative Arts.

REFERENCES

COPYRIGHT LAWS

For those who would like to read the full text of some of the key copyright laws discussed in this book, this section quotes directly from the applicable statutes. (No copyright is claimed in this section.)

17 U.S.C. § 102: Subject matter of copyright

Copyright protection subsists, in accordance with this title, in original works of authorship fixed in any tangible medium of expression, now known or later developed, from which they can be perceived, reproduced, or otherwise communicated, either directly or with the aid of a machine or device. . . . In no case does copyright protection for an original work of authorship extend to any idea, procedure, process, system, method of operation, concept, principle, or discovery, regardless of the form in which it is described, explained, illustrated, or embodied in such work.

17 U.S.C. § 106: Exclusive rights in copyrighted works

[T]he owner of copyright under this title has the exclusive rights to do and to authorize any of the following:

(1) to reproduce the copyrighted work in copies . . .;

(2) to prepare derivative works based upon the copyrighted work;

(3) to distribute copies . . . of the copyrighted work to the public by sale or other transfer of ownership, or by rental, lease, or lending;

. . .

(5) in the case of literary, musical, dramatic, and choreographic works, pantomimes, and pictorial, graphic, or sculptural works, including the individual images of a motion picture or other audiovisual work, to display the copyrighted work publicly . . . .

17 U.S.C. § 412: Registration as prerequisite to certain remedies for infringement

[N]o award of statutory damages or of attorney's fees . . . shall be made for—

(1) any infringement of copyright in an unpublished work commenced before the effective date of its registration; or

(2) any infringement of copyright commenced after first publication of the work and before the effective date of its registration, unless such registration is made within three months after the first publication of the work.

17 U.S.C. § 504: Remedies for infringement: Damages and profits

(a) In General.— Except as otherwise provided by this title, an infringer of copyright is liable for either—

(1) the copyright owner's actual damages and any additional profits of the infringer, as provided by subsection (b); or

(2) statutory damages, as provided by subsection (c).

(b) Actual Damages and Profits.— The copyright owner is entitled to recover the actual damages suffered by him or her as a result of the infringement, and any profits of the infringer that are attributable to the infringement and are not taken into account in computing the actual damages. In establishing the infringer's profits, the copyright owner is required to present proof only of the infringer's gross revenue, and the infringer is required to prove his or her deductible expenses and the elements of profit attributable to factors other than the copyrighted work.

(c) Statutory Damages.—

(1) Except as provided by clause (2) of this subsection, the copyright owner may elect, at any time before final judgment is rendered, to recover, instead of actual damages and profits, an award of statutory damages for all infringements involved in the action, with respect to any one work, for which any one infringer is liable individually, or for which any two or

more infringers are liable jointly and severally, in a sum of not less than $750 or more than $30,000 as the court considers just. For the purposes of this subsection, all the parts of a compilation or derivative work constitute one work.

(2) In a case where the copyright owner sustains the burden of proving, and the court finds, that infringement was committed willfully, the court in its discretion may increase the award of statutory damages to a sum of not more than $150,000. In a case where the infringer sustains the burden of proving, and the court finds, that such infringer was not aware and had no reason to believe that his or her acts constituted an infringement of copyright, the court in its discretion may reduce the award of statutory damages to a sum of not less than $200. The court shall remit statutory damages in any case where an infringer believed and had reasonable grounds for believing that his or her use of the copyrighted work was a fair use under section 107, if the infringer was:

(i) an employee or agent of a nonprofit educational institution, library, or archives acting within the scope of his or her employment who, or such institution, library, or archives itself, which infringed by reproducing the work in copies . . . .

17 U.S.C. § 512: Limitations on liability relating to material online [DMCA Takedown Provisions]

(c) Information Residing on Systems or Networks At Direction of Users.—

(1) In general.— A service provider shall not be liable for monetary relief, or, except as provided in subsection (j), for injunctive or other equitable relief, for infringement of copyright by reason of the storage at the direction of a user of material that resides on a system or network controlled or operated by or for the service provider, if the service provider—

(A) (i) does not have actual knowledge that the material or an activity using the material on the system or network is infringing;

(ii) in the absence of such actual knowledge, is not aware of facts or circumstances from which infringing activity is apparent; or

(iii) upon obtaining such knowledge or awareness, acts expeditiously to remove, or disable access to, the material;

(B) does not receive a financial benefit directly attributable to the infringing activity, in a case in which the service provider has the right and ability to control such activity; and

(C) upon notification of claimed infringement as described in paragraph (3), responds expeditiously to remove, or disable access to, the material that is claimed to be infringing or to be the subject of infringing activity.

(2) Designated agent.— The limitations on liability established in this subsection apply to a service provider only if the service provider has designated an agent to receive notifications of claimed infringement described in paragraph (3), by making available through its service, including on its website in a location accessible to the

public, and by providing to the Copyright Office, substantially the following information:

(A) the name, address, phone number, and electronic mail address of the agent.

(B) other contact information which the Register of Copyrights may deem appropriate.

The Register of Copyrights shall maintain a current directory of agents available to the public for inspection, including through the Internet, and may require payment of a fee by service providers to cover the costs of maintaining the directory.

(3) Elements of notification.—

(A) To be effective under this subsection, a notification of claimed infringement must be a written communication provided to the designated agent of a service provider that includes substantially the following:

(i) A physical or electronic signature of a person authorized to act on behalf of the owner of an exclusive right that is allegedly infringed.

(ii) Identification of the copyrighted work claimed to have been infringed, or, if multiple copyrighted works at a single online site are covered by a single notification, a representative list of such works at that site.

(iii) Identification of the material that is claimed to be infringing or to be the subject of infringing activity and that is to be removed or access to which is to be disabled, and information reasonably sufficient to permit the service provider to locate the material.

(iv) Information reasonably sufficient to permit the service provider to contact the complaining party, such as an address, telephone number, and, if available, an electronic mail address at which the complaining party may be contacted.

(v) A statement that the complaining party has a good faith belief that use of the material in the manner complained of is not authorized by the copyright owner, its agent, or the law.

(vi) A statement that the information in the notification is accurate, and under penalty of perjury, that the complaining party is authorized to act on behalf of the owner of an exclusive right that is allegedly infringed.

. . .

(f) Misrepresentations.— Any person who knowingly materially misrepresents under this section—

(1) that material or activity is infringing, or

(2) that material or activity was removed or disabled by mistake or misidentification,

shall be liable for any damages, including costs and attorneys' fees, incurred by the alleged infringer, by any copyright owner or copyright owner's authorized licensee, or by a service provider, who is injured by such misrepresentation, as the result of the service provider relying upon such misrepresentation in removing or disabling access to the material or activity claimed to be infringing, or in replacing the removed material or ceasing to disable access to it.

(g) Replacement of Removed or Disabled Material and Limitation on Other Liability.—

(1) No liability for taking down generally.— Subject to paragraph (2), a service provider shall not be liable to any person for any claim based on the service provider's good faith disabling of access to, or removal

of, material or activity claimed to be infringing or based on facts or circumstances from which infringing activity is apparent, regardless of whether the material or activity is ultimately determined to be infringing.

(2) Exception.— Paragraph (1) shall not apply with respect to material residing at the direction of a subscriber of the service provider on a system or network controlled or operated by or for the service provider that is removed, or to which access is disabled by the service provider, pursuant to a notice provided under subsection (c)(1)(C), unless the service provider—

(A) takes reasonable steps promptly to notify the subscriber that it has removed or disabled access to the material;

(B) upon receipt of a counter notification described in paragraph (3), promptly provides the person who provided the notification under subsection (c)(1)(C) with a copy of the counter notification, and informs that person that it will replace the removed material or cease disabling access to it in 10 business days; and

(C) replaces the removed material and ceases disabling access to it not less than 10, nor more than 14, business days following receipt of the counter notice, unless its designated agent first receives notice from the person who submitted the notification under subsection (c)(1)(C) that such person has filed an action seeking a court order to restrain the subscriber from engaging in infringing activity relating to the material on the service provider's system or network.

(3) Contents of counter notification.— To be effective under this subsection, a counter notification must be a written communication provided to the service provider's designated agent that includes substantially the following:

(A) A physical or electronic signature of the subscriber.

(B) Identification of the material that has been removed or to which access has been disabled and the location at which the material appeared before it was removed or access to it was disabled.

(C) A statement under penalty of perjury that the subscriber has a good faith belief that the material was removed or disabled as a result of mistake or misidentification of the material to be removed or disabled.

(D) The subscriber's name, address, and telephone number, and a statement that the subscriber consents to the jurisdiction of Federal District Court for the judicial district in which the address is located, or if the subscriber's address is outside of the United States, for any judicial district in which the service provider may be found, and that the subscriber will accept service of process from the person who provided notification under subsection (c)(1)(C) or an agent of such person.

(4) Limitation on other liability.— A service provider's compliance with paragraph (2) shall not subject the service provider to liability for copyright infringement with respect to the material identified in the notice provided under subsection (c)(1)(C).

17 U.S.C. § 1202: Integrity of copyright management information

(b) Removal or Alteration of Copyright Management Information.— No person shall, without the authority of the copyright owner or the law—

(1) intentionally remove or alter any copyright management information,

(2) distribute or import for distribution copyright management information knowing that the copyright management information has been removed or altered without authority of the copyright owner or the law, or

(3) distribute, import for distribution, or publicly perform works, copies of works, or phonorecords, knowing that copyright management information has been removed or altered without authority of the copyright owner or the law,

knowing, or, with respect to civil remedies under section 1203, having reasonable grounds to know, that it will induce, enable, facilitate, or conceal an infringement of any right under this title.

(c) Definition.— As used in this section, the term "copyright management information" means any of the following information conveyed in connection with copies . . . of a work or performances or displays of a work, including in digital form, except that such term does not include any personally identifying information about a user of a work or of a copy, phonorecord, performance, or display of a work:

(1) The title and other information identifying the work, including the information set forth on a notice of copyright.

(2) The name of, and other identifying information about, the author of a work.

(3) The name of, and other identifying information about, the copyright owner of the work, including the information set forth in a notice of copyright.

(4) With the exception of public performances of works by radio and television broadcast stations, the name of, and other identifying information about, a

performer whose performance is fixed in a work other than an audiovisual work. . . .

(6) Terms and conditions for use of the work.

(7) Identifying numbers or symbols referring to such information or links to such information . . . .

OTHER HELPFUL WEBSITES

The Copyright Office maintains many circulars to answer questions you might have about copyright. You can find them online at:

http://www.copyright.gov/circs/.

U.S. federal copyright statutes are available online at sources including

http://www.law.cornell.edu/uscode/.

A number of published copyright cases are available online including by searching "Case law" at http://scholar.google.com/.

ABOUT THE AUTHOR

Christa Laser is an intellectual property litigation attorney at Kirkland & Ellis LLP. Christa has experience counseling clients on copyright law, patent litigation, advertising/promotions law, and other intellectual property concerns. She has litigated intellectual property disputes in federal courts, administrative bodies, and other tribunals. Prior to joining Kirkland, she served as an intern at the U.S. Court of Appeals for the Federal Circuit and the U.S. District Court for the District of Maryland. Christa graduated from the George Washington University Law School with honors, where she was notes editor of the American Intellectual Property Law Association Quarterly Journal and won the world championship of the Manfred Lachs Moot Court Competition.

You can also find her around the web on Facebook, Twitter, and Google+.

Copyright for Photographers

Copyright for Photographers

Copyright for Photographers

www.ingramcontent.com/pod-product-compliance
Lightning Source LLC
Chambersburg PA
CBHW071810170526
45167CB00003B/1256